Blackberry Basics *Recipes*

from Blackberry Farm

JOHN FLEER
Executive Chef

BLACKBERRY FARM PRESS • *Walland, Tennessee*

Contents

II. Blackberry Sweets

III. Blackberry Beverages

Sources

Welcome

At Blackberry Farm, we are in the business of making memories, and our guests tell us our food is among the things they remember most about their visits. Many of the memories I treasure most involve cooking—the gathering of family and friends to share a meal. This, our first cookbook, is a sharing of some of our favorite recipes, with our namesake berries playing an important role in all of them. I hope you have many pleasant moments preparing the selections offered here and that you create your own treasured memories of sharing the enjoyment of them with the special people in your life.

Kreis B. Beall
Proprietress

Because I spent the earliest years of my life at Blackberry Farm, it will always be among the very first places I can remember—associated with smells and tastes and experiences that helped to form my life. And now I have returned to this magical place that means so much to my family and me with my wife Mary Celeste and a child of our own, precious Cameron, who is forming her own memories of Blackberry Farm. The importance of food here cannot be overstated, and now my mission is to bring the marriage of fine wine to that food with vintages that have their own special story, each the product of a time and a place that live on in the wine...and the memories.

Sam Beall
Proprietor

Introduction

We have always shared our recipes at Blackberry Farm, and this cookbook is a response to our guests' interest in the food they have enjoyed during their visits. We launch our first cookbook with our signature blackberry recipes for obvious reasons.

There really are no secrets about cooking and food; it has all been done before. All that we do—or that any other professional kitchen does—is reinterpret and present food in new ways. But a note of thanks from a guest assured us that we are right to publish cookbooks about our style and methods. After thanking us for recipes she received following her stay here and reflecting on her memories of Blackberry Farm, she wrote: "Those who know the most, share the most." While I will certainly not make any claim to knowing the most (I am still learning how to cook), I am gratified to share what I know.

The recipes that follow are an expression of the growth of a certain style of food that I call Foothills Cuisine. The proprietors of Blackberry Farm asked me nine years ago to develop a style of cooking that matched the mission of their country house hotel. Kreis Beall's passion has always been that guests at Blackberry enjoy their visits to our protected mountain setting in comfortable elegance, from the moment they arise from their feather beds to their last bite of dessert by a crackling fire. And now her son, Sam, has joined us to add his passion and love of Blackberry to our guest commitment.

The Blackberry project has been a great challenge, but at the same time the simplest and most natural task I have ever been involved with. I came to Blackberry Farm for three reasons. First, I had been living in the beautiful Hudson Valley of New York while attending culinary school and then working in my first jobs as a culinary graduate. After four years of frozen winter rivers, I was aching to return to my native south. Born and raised in North Carolina, I knew that despite extensive travel throughout my life, my place in the world was somewhere south of the Mason-Dixon. Second, I saw so much potential in this beautiful property. I believed strongly in the mission that the Bealls had set forth for Blackberry Farm. They sought to do what many thought impossible—to combine the genuine charm and simplicity of a country inn nestled in the foothills of the Great Smoky Mountains with the levels of service and amenities to rival the best hotels and resorts around the world. Each guest should experience Blackberry Farm as if it were a visit to his or her own country home. Finally, I came to Blackberry Farm to live for the same reason that so many of our guests continue to return season after season, year after year: the people.

Perfect Food

It did not take long to understand that chief among the "amenities" that Blackberry Farm was to offer was a cuisine that complemented the entire guest experience. This is the type of culinary experience that Sam Beall, Kreis and Sandy's elder son, describes as "perfect" food. Waking up to ripe, fresh fruit and freshly baked breads. Laying down a quilt for a picnic lunch by Hesse Creek. Sipping afternoon tea by the fireplace in the library. Enjoying a candlelight dinner in the Mountain Room. The guest experience at Blackberry is in many ways defined by the food, and to cook native food in this beautiful mountain setting is a simple, natural task.

To achieve the potential of combining that food with the level of service and amenities was the challenge. I returned to one of my fundamental beliefs about cooking: a cuisine or an individual cooking style has nothing if it does not have heart and history. Food is rooted in culture, in memories, and in our experience. For me, Blackberry has become the perfect setting for combining my past experience as a citizen of the South and a traveler of the world with my culinary training. From that union of heart and history, Foothills Cuisine was born. I hope our food at Blackberry Farm and the recipes in this book strike a chord of the familiar in our guests. We are heavily dependent on the foods and traditions of our surrounding South. But I also hope we can bring flashes of the original to our guests, introducing them to foods and techniques they may not have seen in quite this way before and giving them a glimpse of the many links between the table and the garden.

Foothills Cuisine

I use the term Foothills Cuisine in two ways. First, my style of cooking, like the terrain of our setting, is a blend of "high" and "low" cuisine. It is a style of food that wanders the line between refined and rugged, cooking that is a mixture of classical and traditional native methods and foods. Although I am sure that due to the nature of my education, my cooking will always have a touch of the classical and will always depend on fundamental classical techniques, it is also heavily dependent on regional, historical, and family influences. I refer as often to my great-grandmother's treasured recipe book as I do to my classical training.

The other value of the label "Foothills Cuisine" is to locate the home from which the food springs. The foothills of the Great Smoky Mountains and surrounding area are ripe with unique indigenous ingredients, both prepared and fresh. One of the great joys of my job is searching for those special local flavors. Wonderful wild foods—like morels, ramps, and mountain strawberries—and the harvest from our heirloom garden allow us to take advantage of food that cannot be found in any market but that is as close as the hills and fields around us. This is directly reflected in recipes that focus on flavors, seasonality, and a hearty satisfaction of appetite. Foothills food never pretends to intimidate, only to satisfy and nourish.

"The laughter is brightest where the food is best," says an old Irish proverb. Cooking perfect food depends heavily on the intangible ingredient of what I call the "community of the table." While guests enjoy their days and nights at Blackberry Farm, I hope they experience the dining table and the dining room as a place where a community is created that extends beyond the food, where memories are made and rekindled.

JOHN FLEER, *Executive Chef, Blackberry Farm*

How to Cook Perfect Food

I must advise you: the least important part of cooking is the recipe itself. What really matters is its inspiration and spirit. For me, cookbooks are collections of ideas and memories, like a good book of philosophy or fiction. Art is the passion applied to a craft, and cooking is a craft. You make it an art by adding your spirit to the recipes. Restaurant cooking ultimately bears a strong resemblance to classical music, a repetition of a score interpreted in different ways, but always striving for consistency. Cooking at home for friends should be more like jazz. Read the recipe title. Look at the recipe. Now stop, walk away, and close your eyes. Imagine the flavors. Seek out extraordinary ingredients and present them simply, and be flexible. Start cooking. Cook what you have, taste as you cook, and season as you go. Build flavors with layers of taste, and always add that extra dash of spirit. You will achieve perfect food.

JF

Blackberry Savories

Blackberry Plum Soup
with Lime Crème Fraîche

Chilled soups are a refreshing start to a summer dinner or a perfect accompaniment to a crispy salad for a luncheon in the thick heat of a southern summer afternoon. Blackberries and plums converge at the end of the summer. The winey flavors of the plums and the tart sweetness of freshly picked wild blackberries create a fruit soup that is not overly sweet and complements a savory meal. As I suggest below, this soup can be enhanced by a splash (or two) of champagne. I will tell you that the leftover soup makes a wonderfully exotic sauce for vanilla ice cream. *Serves 6.*

Blackberry Plum Soup

Cook plums in sugar and water in a heavy-bottomed 1½-quart saucepan over medium-high heat, stirring occasionally until the liquid has reduced and begins to form thick, pinkish syrup around the plums. Brush down the sides of the pan with a wet pastry brush to prevent sugar crystallization. When the plums' syrup becomes thick, add the blackberry wine, apple juice, and lime juice. Add in blackberries, blackberry puree, and the vanilla bean plus its scrapings.

Stew, covered, over very low heat for half an hour. Remove the vanilla bean pod.

Puree in a blender for one minute until mixture is smooth. Strain through a fine-meshed strainer and chill. This soup will be thick. If you desire, you may dilute it with cider, water, or even some champagne.

Blackberry Puree
Makes 1 cup

Sweat 2 cups of fresh or frozen blackberries over

BLACKBERRY PLUM SOUP

- 1¼ pound or about 7 medium red plums, washed, pitted, medium diced
- ½ cup granulated sugar
- ½ cup water
- ½ cup blackberry wine
- 1½ cups apple cider
- 3 limes, medium, juiced
- 4 cups blackberries
- 1 cup Blackberry Puree (recipe below)
- 1 vanilla bean, split, scraped

BLACKBERRY PUREE
- 2 cups fresh or frozen blackberries

medium-low heat until all of the juices of the black-berries are running free. Puree all in a blender and then strain puree through a fine mesh strainer.

Lime Crème Fraîche

Combine half of the lime zest with the lime juice in a small saucepan or sauté pan. Reduce to almost dry over low heat. Cool to room temperature. Stir lime juice reduction into crème fraîche. Stir remaining lime zest into crème fraîche.

Chef's Note*: The crème fraîche we use as the garnish for this soup is something you can easily make at home as we describe above. You can also buy it in some gourmet markets or you may substitute sour cream. The advantage of crème fraîche is twofold. First the flavor is cleaner than the richness of sour cream, thus making it more suitable for a garnish because it provides a rich but not heavy contrast to this soup and many others. Second, crème fraîche withstands heat better than sour cream, and is therefore excellent for enriching sauces and soups.

Culinary Tip*: Crème fraîche is similar to sour cream but brighter in flavor. To make crème fraîche: Combine 1 cup of heavy cream with 1 tablespoon of butter-milk in a sterile container (i.e. a container that has just come out of the dishwasher) and store in a warm place (close to the oven or on top of the refrigerator) for 2 days. The warming sours the mixture. Refrigerate after 2 days.

Crème fraîche will keep in an airtight container in the refrigerator for 2 weeks.

Ladle 6 ounces of soup into a bowl. Top with 1 tablespoon of lime crème fraîche.

LIME CRÈME FRAÎCHE

3 limes, zested, juiced
1 cup crème fraîche*

Summer Salad
of Honeydew and Blackberries
with Buttermilk Peanut Dressing

This is a great salad for barbeques, summer picnics,
brunches out on the porch, or as a refreshing snack. *Serves 6*

Whisk mayonnaise, buttermilk, and peanut oil
together. Stir in the vinegar, honey, onion powder,
salt, pepper, and peanuts. Adjust with milk to
desired consistency. The consistency should be thick,
but should be thin enough to pour.

Store the dressing in the refrigerator for up to 5
days.

Cut off and discard the rind of the melon, split it
in half, and scoop out and discard the seeds. Cut
each half in half. Trim the ends of each piece, so that
you have squared edges. Thinly slice (⅛-inch thick)
the melon with a sharp knife or on a mandoline.

Toss sliced honeydew melon and blackberries
with the dressing.

Serve this salad in a decorative bowl or if you are
feeling creative, cut another honeydew melon in
half, leaving the rind intact, scoop out and discard
the seeds, and using one half, evenly carve some of
the melon, leaving behind a bowl shape. Fill the
cavity with the salad and serve.

BUTTERMILK PEANUT
DRESSING

¾ cup mayonnaise
1 cup buttermilk
¼ cup roasted peanut oil
¼ cup apple cider vinegar
2 tablespoons honey
1 teaspoon onion powder
½ teaspoon kosher salt
½ teaspoon cracked black
   pepper
1 cup chopped raw
   peanuts

Whole milk
1 honeydew melon
3 pints blackberries

Salad of Mixed Seasonal Greens
with Blackberry Sesame Vinaigrette, Spiced Pecans and a Sesame-Cheddar Wafer

This salad is full of interesting components and contrasting elements. The salad dressing is boldly flavored. The sesame-cheddar wafer and spiced pecans make great snacks unto themselves. With a generous serving of garden greens, extra wafers and pecans, this makes a great "almost lunch" for a hot summer afternoon, leaving plenty of room for cooling ice cream or sorbet or maybe some chocolate buttermilk cake. *Serves 6*

Blackberry Vinegar

Place the blackberries in a quart-size container. Bring the vinegar and the sugar up to a simmer. Simmer until the sugar is dissolved. Pour mixture over blackberries and let cool. Cover tightly and let stand in the refrigerator for several days. Two weeks is the optimum time to allow for flavors to develop in the vinegar. Strain the vinegar through a fine mesh strainer, pressing lightly on the berries. Discard the berry pulp. Store blackberry vinegar in a sealed bottle in the refrigerator. This vinegar will keep for up to a month in the refrigerator.

Blackberry Sesame Vinaigrette

Preheat oven to 350° F.

Combine vinegar, soy sauce, salt and pepper. Combine vegetable oil and sesame oil and whisk into the vinegar mixture. Toast sesame seeds in the oven for 4 to 6 minutes or until golden brown. While still warm, whisk seeds into the vinaigrette.

6 cups mixed seasonal greens
(mesclun mix works well)
6 radishes, cleaned, sliced thin

BLACKBERRY VINEGAR
1½ cups fresh blackberries (frozen may be substituted)
2 cups rice wine vinegar
1 tablespoon sugar

BLACKBERRY SESAME VINAIGRETTE
1 cup Blackberry Vinegar
2 teaspoons soy sauce
½ teaspoon kosher salt
¼ teaspoon cracked black pepper
1¼ cup vegetable oil
½ cup sesame oil
2 tablespoons lightly toasted sesame seeds

4 tablespoons butter
¼ cup granulated sugar
½ cup packed brown
   sugar
½ teaspoon cayenne
   pepper
1 tablespoon water
2 cups shelled, halved
   pecans

Spiced Pecans

Preheat oven to 375° F.

Melt butter in a medium sauté pan over medium heat. Add granulated sugar, brown sugar, and cayenne and cook until sugars dissolve. Add pecans and toss to coat evenly.

Pour all onto a greased cookie sheet and put into the oven for 10 minutes. Remove to greased cooling rack, making sure that as much of the syrup as possible is allowed to drain off.

Store in a tightly sealed container at room temperature for up to 2 weeks. If pecans begin to lose their crunch, pop them back in a 350° F oven for 4 minutes. Watch them carefully. Cool on a greased rack as before.

SESAME-CHEDDAR
WAFER
¼ cup black and white
   sesame seeds
½ stick of unsalted butter,
   room temperature
1 cup shredded extra
   sharp cheddar
1 small egg
½ cup all purpose flour
¼ teaspoon cayenne
   pepper
¼ teaspoon dry mustard
½ teaspoon kosher salt

Sesame-Cheddar Wafer

Preheat oven to 375° F.

Spread sesame seeds on a baking sheet and toast for 10 minutes or until lightly golden in color. Cool.

Cream the butter with the cheese in a mixing bowl with a wooden spoon. Stir in the egg.

Combine sesame seeds, flour, cayenne, mustard, and salt in a separate bowl. Add dry mixture to butter mixture and blend just until all ingredients are incorporated. (You do not want to over mix the dough. This will make wafers tough). Chill the dough for 30 minutes.

Roll out the dough, frequently shifting the dough and adding more flour to prevent it from sticking, on a well-floured surface to 1/16-inch thick. Using a large round ring mold, cut out circles, place on a Silpat* or parchment paper, and bake for 8 to 10 minutes or until light golden brown. Cool. Store tightly covered up to 3 days. Be careful with these wafers, they are delicate!

Salad Assembly

Toss salad greens with Blackberry Sesame Vinaigrette. Season greens with salt and pepper. Place a handful of the dressed greens in the center of the plate in a tight mound. Gently place a Sesame-Cheddar Wafer (benne wafer) on top of the greens. Place a very small amount of dressed greens on top of the wafer. Sprinkle spiced pecans and some thinly sliced radishes around the plate and enjoy. You might even want to garnish this plate with some fresh blackberries.

Chef's Note: This technique for making fruit vinegars applies to all berries. Stone and tree fruits like plums and pears also make excellent fruit vinegars. I prefer to use rice wine vinegar for its light flavor and natural hint of sweetness. If you want to substitute, use white vinegar.

*Culinary Tip: Instead of greasing a baking sheet or using parchment paper, try a Silpat liner. Silpat is a French baking mat that does not stick to anything placed on it. It is a great tool for any kitchen and minimizes the frustration of having your cookies stick relentlessly to your pan.

Blackberry Glazed Quail
Stuffed with Herbed Spoonbread on a Field Pea Salad

Blackberries and game are a natural combination of flavors. In this particular case, boneless quail is marinated in Madeira and shallots, stuffed with an Herbed Spoonbread, and then brushed with a flavorful Blackberry Glaze. I typically serve one quail as an appetizer on a tangy salad of black-eyed peas. Two quail prepared in this fashion would make a most adequate entrée. If you want to introduce blackberries into other game preparation, the glaze is very nice brushed on roasts of venison or elk and can be used with squab just as the quail is prepared. *Serves 6.*

This dish is made up of several recipes. Each recipe, the Quail Marinade, the Blackberry Glaze, Herbed Spoonbread, and the Field Pea Salad, can all be made 1 or 2 days in advance.

Quail Marinade

Examine each quail checking to be sure there are no feathers still attached. Combine Madeira, vegetable oil, shallots, thyme, and pepper. Pour marinade over quail, cover, and refrigerate. Let quail sit in the marinade for 2 to 3 hours. Drain the quail and set aside in the refrigerator.

Blackberry Glaze

Sweat the onion in the butter over low heat until translucent, about 10 minutes. Add garlic and sweat for one minute. Add sugar, Blackberry Puree, water, balsamic vinegar, and soy sauce, and then bring to a simmer. Take mixture off the heat and strain through a fine meshed strainer. Cool thoroughly. Cover and store in the refrigerator for up to 2 weeks.

QUAIL MARINADE
6 quail, semi-boneless, (also called European boneless)
½ cup Madeira wine
¼ cup plus 1 tablespoon vegetable oil
3 shallots, minced
1 teaspoon minced fresh thyme
⅛ teaspoon cracked black pepper

BLACKBERRY GLAZE
¼ cup chopped Vidalia onion
2 tablespoons butter
1 tablespoon chopped garlic
2 tablespoons water
¼ cup sugar
1 cup Blackberry Puree (see page 15)
2 tablespoons balsamic vinegar
2 tablespoons soy sauce

23

2¼ cup whole milk
1 cup plus 1 tablespoon cornmeal
6 tablespoons butter
3 eggs,separated
1½ teaspoons baking powder
1½ teaspoons chopped fresh Italian parsley
1 tablespoon chopped fresh thyme
1½ teaspoon chopped fresh chives
1 teaspoon kosher salt
¼ teaspoon cracked black pepper

Herbed Spoonbread

Preheat oven to 375° F.

Grease a standard 9x5x3-inch loaf pan and set aside.

Bring 1 cup of the milk to a boil. Whisk in cornmeal and butter (mixture should be thick and will separate easily from the sides of the pan) and cook, stirring with a wooden spoon, for 2 to 3 minutes over medium heat. Take cornmeal mixture off the heat and cool to lukewarm.

Beat egg yolks in a separate bowl. Stir the yolks, herbs, salt, and pepper into the cornmeal mixture.

Add the baking powder to the remaining 1 cup milk and stir in the cornmeal mixture.

Beat egg whites to soft peaks in a separate bowl. Gently fold in egg whites into the cornmeal mixture.

Bake in the greased loaf pan for 30 minutes or until a knife in the center comes out clean. If the spoonbread begins to turn too dark, cover it with aluminum foil, and continue baking.

Take spoonbread out of the oven and let it cool. Using a 1 ounce quenelle (egg-shaped) ice-cream scoop or a large tablespoon, portion (1 scoop per person) spoonbread onto a parchment-lined baking sheet. Scoop all spoonbread before stuffing the quail. Refrigerate. The scooped spoonbread will slide easily into the quail cavity once refrigerated.

Field Pea Salad

Soak black-eyed peas in water overnight. Combine vinegars, olive oil, herbs, pepper, and 1 teaspoon salt. Add in diced peppers, green onions, and garlic and let mixture sit covered, overnight.

Drain water from the peas and cook them with the ham hock in chicken stock. Bring peas to a boil, turn down heat, and simmer until beans are tender, about 40 minutes. During the last 10 minutes of cooking add 1 teaspoon salt. Drain, discard ham hock, spread beans, and cool on a baking sheet.

Combine black-eyed peas and dressing. Let sit at room temperature for at least 30 minutes, check the seasoning, adding more salt and pepper if necessary, and then drain excess vinaigrette. Serve at room temperature.

Stuff each portioned spoonbread into the cavity of the quail. Place stuffed quail on a parchment lined baking sheet. Brush the backside of the quail with the blackberry glaze, season with salt and pepper, and then roast the quail for 6 to 8 minutes in a 375°F degree oven. (If you are refrigerating the stuffed quail before roasting, allow the quail to come back up to room temperature before putting them into the oven. Otherwise count on the quail taking 2 minutes longer to cook.) Remove quail from oven and glaze again.

Place about ⅓ cup of field pea salad in the middle of a plate. Place the stuffed quail on top and serve.

Chef's Note: For the best flavor and appearance, brush the glaze on the quail two hours before cooking and then lightly brush again just before cooking. Finally, brush with a coat of blackberry glaze just before serving.

Spoonbread is a Southern specialty that lies between a cornbread pudding and a soufflé. Being hearty, yet light, it is a great complement to quail. As its name implies, it is traditionally to be eaten with a spoon.

FIELD PEA SALAD
1 cup black-eyed peas
1 ham hock
4 cups water

Dressing
3 tablespoons champagne vinegar
3 tablespoons malt vinegar
½ cup olive oil
¾ teaspoon chopped fresh tarragon
½ teaspoon chopped fresh thyme
2½ teaspoons cracked black pepper
1 teaspoon kosher salt
½ red pepper, diced
½ green pepper, diced
½ yellow pepper, diced
2 green onions, thinly sliced
⅓ teaspoon chopped garlic

Blackberry Barbequed Chicken

Pardon the proclamation from this North Carolina boy, but all great barbeque sauce starts with coffee, sorghum, and vinegar. Blackberries and hot peppers complete this spicy, sweet, and tangy sauce. It is excellent on grilled or roasted chicken, but works equally well with all poultry, especially richer birds like quail. For a real Tennessee foothills experience, toss some crispy deep fried frog legs in this sauce. Be generous! *Serves 6*

Blackberry Barbeque Sauce

Caramelize onion in butter in a heavy-bottomed 1-quart saucepan over medium heat, stirring often. If your onions begin to turn too dark, add a little white wine. Add the garlic and jalapeno and continue soaking for 30 seconds. Add the tomato paste and caramelize. Add the tomato paste and caramelize the entire mixture, stirring constantly. (The sugars in the tomato paste will darken. Look for a brick color in the paste.)

Add chili powder, coffee, cider vinegar, sorghum, Worcestershire, balsamic vinegar, blackberry puree, water and soy sauce. Bring mixture up to a boil then simmer all for 30 minutes, stirring occasionally. Strain the sauce through a fine-meshed strainer. Store in refrigerator in an airtight container for up to one week.

Baste Blackberry Barbeque Sauce on chicken either on the grill or roasting in the oven. Don't forget to season the chicken with salt and pepper before applying the barbeque sauce.

1 medium whole chicken, *cut into pieces*

BLACKBERRY BARBEQUE SAUCE

½ medium Vidalia onion, minced
1 tablespoon butter
2 garlic cloves, minced
1 jalapeno pepper, minced
¾ teaspoon ground Chipotle pepper
⅓ cup + 1 tablespoon tomato paste
1 tablespoon chili powder
½ cup + 2 tablespoons brewed coffee
¼ cup apple cider vinegar
¼ cup sorghum
2 tablespoons Worcestershire sauce
2 tablespoons balsamic vinegar
½ cup Blackberry Puree (see page 15)
2 tablespoons water
1½ teaspoons soy sauce

Chef's Note: You will see sorghum, also called sorghum molasses, in many of my recipes. Sorghum is a native ingredient, still primarily crafted by hand in the Appalachian region by extracting the sap from tall, indigenous cane and gently cooking it to a sweet syrup. Beyond the fact that it is native to these foothills, I think it adds a beautiful, unique, floral complexity to many recipes, both sweet and savory. Please do not substitute blackstrap molasses for sorghum in any of our recipes. If you must, you can make a stand-in by combining three parts honey to one part blackstrap molasses.

Blackberry Wine Marinated Veal Chop
with White Bean and Sundried Tomato Ragout, Collard Greens, and Roasted Shallot and Garlic Sauce

Serves 6

Blackberry Wine Marinade

Combine the blackberry wine, olive oil, shallots, rosemary, and pepper. Pour over oven-ready veal chops. Cover tightly and let veal chops sit in the marinade, refrigerated, for 24 hours.

Culinary Tip: Two tablespoons blackberry brandy mixed with 1 cup red wine can be substituted for blackberry wine.

White Bean and Sundried Tomato Ragout

Soak dried beans overnight in water.

Sauté country ham in vegetable oil in a heavy-bottomed 2-quart saucepan over medium heat until golden brown, stirring frequently. Add onions and cook until soft, following with carrots and celery and cooking until tender, continuing to stir often. Drain the water from the beans. Add beans, chicken stock, cayenne pepper, salt, and pepper. Bring the beans to a boil, and then turn down heat to a simmer. Simmer, uncovered, until beans are cooked thoroughly, 1 hour to 1½ hours, stirring occasionally. Stir in julienned sun-dried tomatoes in the last 10 minutes of cooking. Taste the beans. Add more salt and pepper if necessary.

BLACKBERRY WINE MARINADE
1½ cups blackberry wine*
1½ cups olive oil
2 tablespoons chopped shallots
2 tablespoons chopped fresh rosemary
¼ teaspoon cracked black pepper

WHITE BEAN AND SUNDRIED TOMATO RAGOUT
½ pound (1¼ cups) dried white beans
1 country ham slice (2"x2"), diced
1 tablespoon vegetable oil
1 medium white onion, diced
½ medium carrot, peeled, diced
½ stalk celery, diced
1 quart chicken stock
1 pinch cayenne pepper
¾ teaspoon kosher salt
To taste cracked black pepper
½ cup julienne sun-dried tomatoes

1 tablespoon olive oil
2 pounds collard greens,
stems removed,
washed, chopped
White wine
1 teaspoon kosher salt
¼ teaspoon cracked
black pepper

Culinary Tip: The country ham brings additional salt to these beans. If you are using canned beans take into account the possible added salt in the can. Just remember to always taste, taste, taste and your beans will be perfect.

Collard Greens

Bring a large pot of salted water to a rolling boil. Drop the collards in the boiling water and let them blanch for 5 minutes. Remove collards and immediately drop them in a large bowl of ice water. Let the collards cool, and then drain and pat dry. Heat a large sauté pan with 1 tablespoon of olive oil to medium-high heat, about 30 seconds. Add collards, turning the greens over in the pan constantly. Add a little white wine to quicken the cooking process. Add a pinch of salt and pepper. Sauté the greens until they are fully cooked and heated through, about 2 minutes.

Culinary Tip: The collards can be blanched 1 day in advance. Just store them covered in the refrigerator.

ROASTED SHALLOT AND
GARLIC SAUCE
9 shallots, peeled
olive oil
2 garlic bulbs
kosher salt
cracked black pepper
½ cup blackberry wine
1½ cups veal jus

Roasted Shallot and Garlic Sauce

Preheat the oven to 325° F.

Make sure all shallots are approximately the same size. Toss the shallots in enough olive oil just to lightly coat. Place in a sauté pan or shallow baking pan and roast, uncovered, in the oven for 10 minutes. After 10 minutes toss the shallots and continue to roast them for an additional 10 minutes, less or more, depending on their size. The shallots should be golden brown in color and soft. Let the shallots cool to room temperature.

Toss the garlic bulbs in enough olive oil to coat. Place them in a small pan and roast for 30 minutes.

Take out of the oven and let cool at room temperature. Cut the top of the bulb off with a sharp knife and squeeze the roasted cloves out of the bulb.

Reduce the blackberry wine with the shallots and garlic until almost dry. Stir in the veal jus and bring to a simmer. Season to taste with salt and pepper. Stir in the roasted shallots and garlic. Keep sauce warm over low heat.

To Assemble

Preheat the grill to high heat.

Preheat the oven to 350° F.

Remove the veal chop from the marinade. Season both sides of the veal chops with salt and pepper. Grill on both sides for 1 to 2 minutes. Remove from the grill into a medium sauté pan, and place the chop in the oven to finish cooking for 4 to 5 minutes (to medium-rare).

Sauté greens as mentioned in above recipe.

Portion ½ cup of the white bean and sundried tomato ragout in the center of the plate. Encircle the collard greens tightly around the beans. Set the veal chop over the beans at an angle. Drizzle the sauce in a circle around the outside of the greens. Garnish with fresh blackberries.

Chef's Note: Veal Jus is a restaurant luxury with a lot of work behind it. It starts with fifty pounds of veal bones and ends with 2 gallons of rich meat essence— liquid gold. You can purchase this in small containers at many gourmet markets now or see our source listing for Summerfield Farm. You can mail order reduced veal stock in larger quantities from them.

Blackberry Memories

Some of my earliest memories from childhood include summer days spent picking blackberries. I vividly recall the scent of oil of citronella which was used as a mosquito repellant and a sulphur compound which was rubbed on the skin to ward off chig. while were picking berries in the Blackberry cane thickets.

In late June or early July I would spend time picking berries with the adults for my grandmothers use in the making of blackberry jelly.

Needless to say, on many occasions more of the berries found there way into my mouth than into the bucket

Most of my knowledge concerning blackberries came from old timers that I have known here in the mountains of East Tennessee over the years. One of the many welcome sights of spring are the white blossoms of blackberries in full bloom along roadsides, fencerows, thickets in pastures, and at the edge of woodland areas. Those who pick blackberries for culinary purposes follow there stages of development with a keen interest. The berries first appear in a green stage of development, later changing to white, then red, and finally to black at which stage they are ready for picking.

Years ago I knew a great number of people in the country who subsisted almost entirely on what they raised and gathered from the wild. Blackberries were an important staple for winter use along with other canned fruits which were used in the making of cobblers and pies.

I have seen roofing tin covered with blackberries drying in the hot summer sun.

When the berries were dry they were stored in sacks and hung from the rafters until they were needed for use during during the winter months. As needed, the berries were soaked in water until they were fully re-constituted, and then used in the recipe that called for them.

The berries were also canned fresh. I can remember the filled jars being processed in copper canning tubs over an open fire.

In our mountains of east Tennessee blackberries have been most noted for four things. I can't recall a time of coming in for the noon "dinner" during late summer's tobacco cutting season and not having blackberry cobbler

As part of the large meal being served.

Blackberry cobbler made with wild blackberries has a distinct unique flavor which can not come close to being duplicated by blackberries which are large in size, seed, and lacking in flavor. Then there are the blackberry jams and jellies which are made during the picking season. The jars filled with these jams and jellies are a beautiful sight lined up on pantry shelves awaiting there use during the cold winter months. One of my favorite things are hot homemade biscuits served with blackberry jelly.

Then there is blackberry wine which is still made by a number of people in the country and enjoyed by the family and given as gifts at christmas time.

No discussion of blackberries would be complete without mentioning blackberry winter, which is one of spring's last cold spells, along with dogwood and whippoorwill winter.

John Coykendall,
Heirloom gardener at
Blackberry Farm

Doing it Right

"Always do right. This will gratify some people and astonish the rest." That is Mark Twain's version of The Golden Rule, and I think its sentiment has been the key to our success over the last decade. It is not the mantra of the perfectionist but a simple philosophy executed in a beautiful place that our guests describe as Camelot, Valhalla, and Heaven on Earth. Kreis has stated her own version of what it means to do right. She has often said "The main thing for anybody to know is this: there is no right or wrong way. It's the spirit behind the effort that becomes memory." Blackberry is a country home where we welcome guests to a place where things can be done right, where the spirit of the property creates memories. Our guests find themselves equipped with all the tools for a great day, whatever their chosen balance of activity and rest, and they call it a beautiful place. Our staff applies the golden rule with genuine care, and guests call it a great service. We hire tremendous people, treat them well and allow them to grow, and they call it a great place to work. We cook food the way it should be—regionally inspired, fresh, created with heart and soul—and it is called great cuisine. There is still a place where the world is that simple.   JF

Blackberry Sweets

Hearty Blackberry Jam

The best thing about great jam is preserving the essence of the fruit
at its peak of flavor. The second best thing about a great jam is that you can
recognize that it was actually borne of that fruit. This jam has a wonderful
balance of sweet syrup essence of blackberry and hearty bits of fruit. With this
flavor and texture you won't forget what you are eating. Unquestionably best on
warm, lightly buttered toast. Our proprietors, the Beall family, have a "secret
sandwich" which consists of toast, jam, and nice, crisp bacon. Now that
the secret is out, try it out with this jam first.
Makes 2 quarts.

Hearty Blackberry Jam

Blackberries should be at room temperature.

Combine 1 cup sugar with 1 box of pectin.
Set aside.

Pick off the stems of the blackberries and place
in a 2 quart heavy-bottomed saucepan over
medium-high heat. Stir blackberry wine into the
blackberries and slowly bring the mixture to a boil.

Add the lemon juice and zest and simmer 8 to 10
minutes.

Remove whole fruit with a slotted spoon and put
into half-pint or pint airtight containers. Simmer
juice rapidly, stirring occasionally and skimming
foam from the edge, until it is reduced by half and
beginning to thicken. At this point add the remaining sugar and bring it to a boil. Immediately reduce
the heat to a simmer. Cook until the consistency
begins to be syrupy and the juice forms short
streams when dropped from a spoon. If the juice
sheets from spoon, the jam will be too stiff.

Once reduced, whisk in pectin-sugar mixture.
Stir continuously until mixture reaches a boil, and

BLACKBERRY JAM

- 7 cups granulated sugar
- 1 box powdered fruit pectin
- 2 quarts blackberries, crushed
- 1 cup blackberry wine
- 2 teaspoons lemon juice
- 1 teaspoon lemon zest
- 2 tablespoons unsalted butter

1½ cups Hearty
  Blackberry Jam
1 cup blackberries,
  coarsely chopped
3 teaspoons black,
  green, and white
  peppercorns, *coarsely
  chopped
3 each green onions,
  chopped
2 oranges, medium,
  zested and juiced
1 tablespoon balsamic
  vinegar
2 tablespoons fresh basil
  leaves, chopped
1 tablespoon brandy
Pinch of kosher salt

then simmer for 1 minute. Take off heat, stir in butter to melt and pour over the fruit in the airtight containers. Cool. Cover and let stand at room temperature 24 hours to set.

Store containers in freezer for up to 1 year. Jam can be stored in refrigerator for up to 3 weeks.

Blackberry Peppercorn Relish

Makes 1½ pints

Use this Hearty Blackberry Jam in the form of a spicy relish. This zesty peppercorn relish will add a sweet zing to any summer game or meat dish.

Chop orange zest.

Mix jam, blackberries, peppercorns, green onions, orange zest, orange juice, vinegar, basil, and brandy together, season with salt and chill. Store in an airtight container. The relish will keep for up to 2 weeks in the refrigerator. Serve at room temperature.

Culinary Tip: To coarsely chop the peppercorns, use the back of a heavy sauté pan and gently crush the peppercorns on a non-scratch surface or use a mortar and pestle. Pulsing the peppercorns in a coffee bean grinder works well, too.

Sally Lunn Bread

Sally Lunn Bread is an English tradition that has been adopted by the South. This is simple brioche-like bread with a tender crumb. Sliced thick and filled with fresh strawberries, Sally Lunn makes a great French Toast, but like all bread it is best fresh out of the oven lightly dressed with soft butter or homemade blackberry jam. *Makes 1 loaf.*

Bring sugar and milk to a boil to dissolve sugar. When mixture reaches a boil, stir in the cubed butter. Completely melt butter. Remove mixture from the stove and cool to lukewarm.

Proof yeast in warm water for 5 minutes. Place yeast and water in a warm place. Add to the lukewarm milk mixture and let stand until frothy.

Combine milk-yeast mixture and eggs in a mixing bowl. Combine flour and salt and add the dry ingredients all at once to the wet.

Mix on low speed until the dough comes together. Adjust consistency with additional flour if necessary. Dough should clean the sides of the bowl. Knead an additional 5 minutes on medium-low speed.

Transfer dough to a large, lightly oiled bowl. Lightly oil the top of the dough, cover with plastic wrap, and allow to stand in a warm place until doubled in volume.

Punch down dough and turn out onto a lightly floured surface. Shape into a loaf and place in a greased loaf pan. Allow to stand until almost doubled. Gently split the top of the loaf lengthwise with a serrated knife or a razor blade.

Bake at 375° F for 45 to 50 minutes. Turn out on cooling rack. Wrap tightly in plastic wrap and store in the freezer for up to 2 weeks.

SALLY LUNN BREAD
- 3 tablespoons granulated sugar
- 1 cup whole milk
- 6 tablespoons butter cubed, room temperature
- 1 tablespoon dry active yeast
- ¼ cup water, warmed to 100 to 115° F
- 3 eggs, large, at room temperature
- 1½ teaspoons kosher salt
- 6½ cups all-purpose flour

Blackberry Twists

These easy pastries make for a great breakfast pastry or a simple light dessert with ice cream. They are especially good with our bourbon white chocolate ice cream. Try this same method with savory fillings like cream cheese and herbs, or spice them up with cayenne pepper and Parmesan cheese. You should not feel any shame in using pre-made puff pastry. Everybody else does! *Serves 6.*

BLACKBERRY TWISTS
- 3 tablespoons cake crumbs*
- ¼ cup light brown sugar
- ½ teaspoon cinnamon, *ground*
- ¼ teaspoon kosher salt
- 1 frozen puff pastry sheet, slightly thawed
- 4 tablespoons blackberry jam, seedless
- 1 egg
- 2 tablespoons heavy cream

Preheat the oven to 425° F.

Mix the cake crumbs, brown sugar, cinnamon, and salt. On a lightly floured flat surface, roll puff pastry to half its original thickness (about ⅛" thick and 1' by 1'). Trim edges. Spread the blackberry jam over the bottom horizontal half of the puff pastry. Sprinkle the cake crumbs-brown sugar mix over jam.

Fold the top of the puff pastry over the coated bottom layer. Roll lightly with the rolling pin to flatten slightly and create a better stick of puff pastry. Whisk egg and heavy cream together. Brush egg wash over the puff pastry. Cut the dough from top to bottom into 1" wide strips using a knife or a dough cutter. Holding onto both ends of each strip, twist twice, lay on a parchment-lined sheet tray with about 1" space in between each one, and bake in a 425° F oven, for 10 to 12 minutes or until golden brown. Cool. Remove from parchment and serve.

Culinary Tip: Plain breadcrumbs can be substituted for the cake crumbs.

Blackberry Picnic Pound Cake

This is a very flavorful, dense pound cake, making it perfect for picnics. Enjoy this at room temperature. Do not refrigerate it. You can't taste that pound of butter when the cake is cold! Also try this pound cake toasted with some homemade vanilla ice cream. *1 Loaf*

Preheat oven to 325° F.

Grease a standard 9x5x3-inch loaf pan with shortening or butter.

Cream the butter and sugar, scraping often, until very light and fluffy. Mixture should double.

Break eggs into a container with a pourable spout. (Breaking the eggs first into a different container insures that no egg shells fall into your cake batter. If you do have some break, use a broken piece of shell to scoop it out. The shells attract each other.)

Add up to 6 eggs, several at a time, to butter and sugar mixture on low speed, scraping often. After adding 6 eggs, mix in 1 cup of flour. (The flour helps prevent the mixture from breaking and looking curdled. When the mixture breaks, volume is lost.) Add the remaining 2 eggs.

Pour in the vanilla and brandy, continuing to mix on low speed.

Add remaining flour in three batches, mixing on low speed. Scrape bottom of bowl, making sure all ingredients have been evenly incorporated.

Divide the mixture in half. Fold the warmed preserves into half of the batter.

Fill two *piping bags. (If cloth piping bags are unavailable, use a disposable piping bag or a resealable plastic bag. If using the plastic bag, just fill it

BLACKBERRY PICNIC POUND CAKE

- 4 sticks (1 pound) unsalted butter, room temperature
- 2¼ cups (1 pound) sugar
- 8 eggs, room temperature
- 4 cups (1 pound) unsifted all purpose flour
- 1½ teaspoons iodized salt
- ¾ teaspoon vanilla extract
- 2 tablespoons blackberry brandy
- ¼ cup seedless blackberry preserves, warmed

about two-thirds full, twist the opened end, then cut a tip with some scissors at one corner of the bag and pipe away. Your tip needs to be ½-inch wide.)

Pipe four alternating stripes on the bottom of the greased loaf pan. The stripes should be tall and fat and should cover the entire bottom of the pan.

Repeat piping on the next layer, reversing the color order; pipe purple on top of white, etc.

Repeat on the third (maybe fourth) layer until pan is NO MORE THAN THREE-QUARTERS FULL. There may be a small amount of batter left, so let the kids lick the bowl, bake off a mini cake, or have a snack!

Bake in a 325°F oven for approximately 1 hour and 45 minutes. Test the cake with a toothpick or knife. If it comes out clean it is ready to come out.

Invert on a rack and let cool. Store tightly wrapped at room temperature.

Variation: Any type of brandy or jam will work in this recipe, so be creative.

*Chef's Note: Using a pastry bag can be an unpleasant and messy experience if "piping" is not an everyday practice. Here are a couple of tips that will bring every novice and expert piping success.

1. Always choose the right size bag for the right size task. Do not overfill. It is better to under fill.

2. When filling the bag, first fold down the top third of the bag, like a cuff.

While holding the bag with one hand directly underneath the cuff, fill the bag with your pound cake batter up to the cuff mark. Unfold the cuff and twist the opening closed. Hold the twisted top with one hand and squeeze while guiding the tip with the other hand.

Blackberry "Biscuits and Gravy"

Though a native southerner, I think I am missing the gene that makes me love traditional sausage or sawmill gravy. This adaptation is a bold sweet beginning to your day with the same "elbows on the table" appeal of its heavier cousin. Make sure you spread your Lemon Shortcake with plenty of butter. The flavors of the sorghum, warm blackberries and butter are just right. *Serves 6.*

Lemon Shortcake

Preheat oven to 400° F.

Combine lemon zest and sugar in a food processor. Process until zest is finely chopped. Add flour, baking powder, and salt. Pulse to mix evenly. Cut butter into food processor and pulse several times until the mixture resembles coarse meal.

Remove dry ingredients to a large mixing bowl. Whisk 2 eggs, milk, and cream together in a separate mixing bowl. Add wet ingredients to the dry and stir to combine.

Roll out the dough on a lightly floured surface to ¾-inch thick. Cut rounds with a 2-inch wide fluted cutter and place cakes 1-inch apart on a parchment-lined baking sheet. Beat the other egg with a tablespoon of water in a small mixing bowl. Brush this egg wash on the tops of the shortcakes. Sprinkle cakes with rock sugar.

Bake for 10 to 12 minutes. The shortcakes will be lightly browned and the centers should spring back. The shortcakes will keep for one day in a tightly covered container.

LEMON SHORTCAKE
Makes 6 cakes

- 3 tablespoons granulated sugar
- 1 lemon, zested
- 3⅓ cup White Lily flour (cake flour)
- 1½ tablespoons baking powder
- 1½ teaspoons kosher salt
- 4½ ounces (1 stick plus 1 tablespoon) unsalted butter, cold
- 3 eggs
- ½ cup whole milk
- ¼ cup heavy cream
- 1 tablespoon lemon juice
- 3 tablespoons rock sugar

"GRAVY"

Makes 3 cups

1½ quarts fresh or frozen blackberries

3 tablespoons granulated sugar

½ cup sorghum

¾ tablespoon lemon juice

2 tablespoons plus 2 teaspoons blackberry wine (or fruit juice)

3 tablespoons arrowroot

"Gravy"

Cook half of the berries, the granulated sugar, sorghum, lemon juice, and blackberry wine over medium heat for about 10 minutes or until the berries begin to release their juice.

Strain 2 tablespoons of the released juices from the berries into a small mixing bowl. Whisk the arrowroot into the strained juice to form a slurry. Whisk slurry into the cooked berries.

Increase the heat to medium-high and bring berries to a simmer. Simmer for 2 to 3 minutes, stirring constantly. Remove from the heat and hold warm. Fold in remaining berries just before serving.

To serve, ladle approximately 1 cup of blackberries and "gravy" over a warm lemon shortcake spread liberally with sweet butter. Top with a large dollop of whipped sweetened cream.

Chef's Note: Arrowroot is a much purer thickener than cornstarch. Unfortunately it is not as easy to obtain. Look in the spice section at the grocery store or your local health food store. If necessary you may substitute cornstarch. The term "slurry" refers to a loose paste made with a cool liquid and the arrowroot. Make sure to start with the arrowroot and stir in the liquid. Your index finger is the best tool for this job.

Blackberry Sorbet
on Oven-Roasted Peaches

A great ending to a simple summer meal. If you don't have an ice cream
machine, do as the resourceful Italians do and make granite, by placing the
blackberry syrup in a shallow container in the freezer and stirring about every 20
to 30 minutes until you have blackberry "ice". Roasting stone fruits like peaches
or plums truly bring a wonderful depth of flavor to the table. This
combination is hard to beat finishing your meal, sitting on the
back porch watching the fireflies. *Serves 6.*

Blackberry Sorbet
Makes 2 quarts

Boil blackberries in water for 30 seconds. Puree
berries and juice in a blender. Strain the berry puree
through a small-holed strainer, pushing against the
sides with the back of a small ladle, forcing the pulp
through.

Add sugar to the pulp and juice and bring to a
boil, constantly stirring. Simmer until sugar has
dissolved, about one minute. Take the mixture off of
the heat. Stir in corn syrup. Cool to room
temperature.

Freeze in an ice cream machine according to the
manufacturer's instructions. The sorbet will have the
consistency of soft-serve ice cream. Immediately eat
or store in the freezer.

Oven-Roasted Peaches

Preheat oven to 450° F.

Place peaches, skin-side down, in a shallow
greased baking dish. Brush melted butter on

BLACKBERRY SORBET
2 pints blackberries
3 cups water
2 cups granulated sugar
½ cup light corn syrup

OVEN-ROASTED
PEACHES
6 peaches, ripe, halved,
   pit removed
1 cup melted butter
2 tablespoons brown
   sugar
1 teaspoon ground
   nutmeg

peaches. Mix brown sugar with nutmeg and sprinkle on peaches.

Roast the peaches for 4 minutes or until they are golden brown. For a deeper caramelization, broil the peaches for about 4 minutes instead of roasting them.

Serve the warm peaches with scoops of the Blackberry Sorbet.

Variations: This sorbet can be made with a variety of different fruits. Just remember to taste the fruit before adding the sugar. Some fruits are sweeter than others and can change sweetness depending on the season, the size of the fruit, and its ripeness. Blackberries are a rather tart fruit, thus needing a larger amount of sugar to bring out its natural flavor.

Chef's Note: I may be committing a horrible crime against the guild of chefs by revealing the secret to great ice creams and sorbets, but here it is. Inverted sugar, or more simply, liquid sweeteners like corn syrup and honey, are essential to the "creamy" texture of restaurant sorbets and ice creams. Don't tell anyone you read this here. It doesn't take much, but it makes a big difference.

Blackberry Fool in Oatmeal Lace

The lazy southern tongue has blessed us with this lazy adaptation
of the classic English Trifle (Try-Fool). This dish is a wonderfully simple dessert
that depends only on your ability to whip cream and find the best, sweetest
blackberries. I have provided this recipe in its simplest form. If you are feeling
whimsical or creative you can certainly add spices like clove or allspice or
cinnamon to the blackberries as they are cooking or even fresh herbs. Fresh sage
makes for an interesting combination. You can even mix the berries
with other seasonal fruit. *Serves 6.*

BLACKBERRY FOOL
2½ cups fresh, sweet
    blackberries
½ cup granulated sugar
1 cup heavy cream
1 tablespoon brown
    sugar

OATMEAL LACE COOKIE
¾ cup oatmeal
½ stick plus 1 tablespoon
    butter
¼ cup plus 1 tablespoon
    light corn syrup
⅔ cup packed brown
    sugar
¾ cup all purpose flour

Blackberry Fool

Cook ⅓ cup of blackberries in sugar and water
over medium heat until tender. Increase heat to
high to evaporate water. Cook until syrup has
formed.

Immediately toss in remaining berries. Remove
from heat, cover, and let stand 15 minutes.

Drain syrup and reserve. Let strained fruit cool.
When the fruit has cooled, stir fruit to make a
chunky puree.

Whip the cream with the brown sugar to form
moist firm peaks. Fold in strained blackberry puree.
Chill for 30 minutes before serving.

Oatmeal Lace Cookie

Chop oatmeal in a food processor until flakes are
broken up but not powdered. Set aside. Melt butter
in a small saucepan. Add corn syrup and brown
sugar, and then bring mixture to a boil. Remove
from the heat. Stir in the oatmeal and flour. Cool to
room temperature.

Preheat oven to 375° F.

Using a small cookie scoop or a tablespoon, drop cookie dough onto a well-greased baking sheet about 4 inches apart on all sides. Place into the oven and bake 7 to 10 minutes or until golden brown. The cookies will flatten while baking. They are done when the dough stops bubbling. Let the cookies cool for a moment before removing them from the pan. They are too delicate to handle right out of the oven.

Quickly place the cookies over an upside down soup bowl and let cool until the cookie is hard. Please be careful, the cookies will be hot.

Chef's Note: This is a dessert that is best presented very simply. Other than a big crisp oatmeal lace cookie, my favorite is in a big martini glass with fresh picked wild blackberries, a little bit of the syrup drizzled over the fool and a big sprig of fragrant garden mint.

You may well end up with extra syrup. Save it and use it for syrup on your Sunday morning pancakes.

Culinary Tip: Any type mold such as a soup bowl, a can, a jar, etc. can be used to shape these cookies. Just remember to work quickly so that the cookie remains pliable and warm while you are molding it.

Variation: For a delectable low-fat version of the Blackberry Fool, just follow the preparation below.

Low-Fat Blackberry Fool with a Lemon Tuile

Prepare the yogurt cheese 1 day or 6 hours in advance. See following culinary tip.

Cook ⅓ cup blackberries in water with sugar, nutmeg, and a cheesecloth bag of the peppercorns and cloves over medium heat until tender.

LOW-FAT BLACKBERRY FOOL
1½ cups fresh blackberries
1½ tablespoons water
3 tablespoons brown sugar
5 white whole peppercorns
Pinch of fresh ground nutmeg
2 whole cloves
6 ounces nonfat *yogurt cheese, room temperature
¾ cup Swiss meringue

Increase the heat to high to evaporate water. Cook until syrup has formed. Remove the spice bag.

Immediately toss remaining berries into the cooked berry mixture. Remove from the heat, cover, and let stand 15 minutes. Drain syrup and reserve. Let the fruit cool.

When cool, stir the fruit with a wooden spoon to make a chunky puree.

Fold in room temperature yogurt cheese into Swiss Meringue. Fold in Blackberry Puree.

Serve with fresh blackberries, a drizzle of the reserved syrup, and a lemon tuile or any other delicate cookie.

Swiss Meringue

Whip 3 egg whites with 1 cup sugar in small mixing bowl over a simmering water bath until the sugar dissolves and the temperature reaches 125° F. (feels like a hot bath).

Immediately attach the bowl to the mixer, add cream of tartar, and whip at high speed for about 15 minutes. You can whip this indefinitely, but once you turn it off don't whip it again. It will deflate.

Lemon Tuile

This batter must be refrigerated 24 hours in advance before baking.

Combine the confectioner's sugar and flour. Stir in melted butter and lemon juice until batter is smooth. Cover and refrigerate for 24 hours.

Preheat oven to 400° F.

Remove batter from the refrigerator and allow it to come to room temperature. Spread 1 teaspoon of the batter on a nonstick cookie sheet (or a

Silpat-lined sheet) as thinly as possible in the shape of a circle with a small offset spatula. You may also use a circular template cut from plastic to form the circles. Repeat until your cookie sheet is full. Bake tuiles for 7 minutes, or until the cookies are golden brown and lacy.

Remove cookies from the oven and let cookies rest for a minute. Remove them from the pan with a small spatula or butter knife and mold each cookie into a small cup or bowl, or roll into a cigarette shape with your fingers. Be creative, yet be careful because the cookie may be hot and tuiles are very fragile. Set aside and let cool. Remove from the molds and use within 1 day. Store in an airtight container until ready to use.

Culinary Tip: Yogurt Cheese is simply yogurt drained of its water content. Just pour out a container of non-fat plain yogurt into some cheesecloth and tightly tie the open ends into a knot. Suspend the cheese over a container (to catch the yogurt liquid) and allow it to hang for at least 6 hours and up to 24 hours maximum. It can be flavored wit herbs, spices, roasted peppers, etc. It is a great low-fat alternative to cream cheese and can be used in savory and sweet dishes.

Chocolate Buttermilk Cake
with Blackberry Jam and Bourbon Whipped Cream

Chocolate and blackberries wonderfully complement each other in this simple cake recipe. This is a fitting finish to a summer barbeque and can be made a day ahead, and frosted before served. You could leave the bourbon out of the whipped cream icing, but you will be sorry you did. *1 cake.*

Chocolate Buttermilk Cake

Preheat the oven to 375° F.

Coat two 9-by-2-inch round cake pans with vegetable oil, spray and line the bottoms with parchment paper. Lightly spray the paper.

In a large bowl, sift together the flour, sugar, cocoa, baking soda and salt.

Whisk Blackberry Puree, buttermilk, oil, vinegar and vanilla together in a large mixing bowl. Whisk dry ingredients into wet ingredients in thirds. Stir to just incorporate the dry and wet ingredients evenly. DO NOT OVERMIX.

Divide the batter evenly between the prepared pans, shake, and gently knock the bottoms of the pans (to shake out air bubbles and to evenly spread cake batter). Bake for about 40 minutes, or until the cakes pull away from the sides and the tops spring back when pressed. Let cool on a rack for 10 minutes, then unmold the cakes and cool completely. Divide each layer in half horizontally using a long serrated knife.

Spread Blackberry Jam between layers, using 1 cup on each layer.

CHOCOLATE
BUTTERMILK CAKE
vegetable oil spray
3 cups all-purpose flour
2 cups sugar
¾ cup cocoa powder, unsweetened, Dutch process
2 teaspoons baking soda
1 teaspoon salt
1 cup Blackberry Puree (see page 15)
1 cup buttermilk, low-fat (1.5%)
⅔ cup vegetable oil
2 tablespoons vinegar, distilled white
2 teaspoons vanilla
1½ cup Hearty Blackberry Jam, room temperature (see page 41 or substitute any high quality jam with texture)

Bourbon Whipped Cream Icing

Combine whipping cream, sugar, and bourbon.

Whip until medium peaks form. Spread generously on the sides and top of the Chocolate Buttermilk Cake.

Garnish with fresh berries and mint sprigs.

Keep this cake covered and refrigerated. This cake is best when eaten the day it is made or the day after.

Chef's Note: The chocolate cake here is not only simple, but also very versatile. Make extra batter, bake all of the cakes and freeze some of the layers for a spontaneous summer party.

BOURBON WHIPPED CREAM
- 2 cups heavy whipping cream
- ⅓ cup confectioner's sugar
- ⅓ cup bourbon

Blackberry Streusel Tart

This tart is a perfect example of the blend between the fancy
and the familiar in our Foothills Cuisine. A streusel tart is one of the most
simple, rustic form of fruit pies. However, buried inside this seemingly
straightforward tart is a surprising layer of vanilla-scented mascarpone cheese.
Once you pair this tart with one of our favorite ice creams, Bourbon White
Chocolate, you have quite the summer dessert. *One 9-inch tart.*

This recipe contains several different components,
each of which can be made in advance.

Sweet Pastry Dough

Combine all-purpose flour, granulated sugar,
salt, and baking powder. Cut in butter with a knife.
Blend butter into dry ingredients using the heels of
your hands until the mixture resembles coarse meal
or grated Parmesan cheese. Stir in one egg and press
into a ball. Let dough rest in refrigerator for 1 hour.
This recipe will make enough dough for one tart.
This dough can be made in advance and frozen for
up to one month. If frozen, allow dough to thaw in
the refrigerator overnight.

Preheat oven to 375° F.

If you are using frozen pie dough, disregard the
first section concerning the Sweet Pastry Dough.
Begin the recipe with the tart bottom layer and pro-
ceed from there.

Vanilla-Mascarpone Layer

Scrape the insides of the vanilla bean and add to
mascarpone cheese into a small bowl. Beat in egg.
Refrigerate if not using right away. This mixture
will hold in the refrigerator for 2 days.

SWEET PASTRY DOUGH
- 1 cup White Lily all-purpose flour
- ¼ cup granulated sugar
- Pinch of salt
- ¼ teaspoon baking powder
- ½ stick unsalted butter, small diced
- 1 egg, beaten

VANILLA-MASCARPONE
LAYER
1 cup mascarpone
   cheese
1 vanilla bean
1 egg

TART FILLING
4 cups fresh (frozen
   blackberries can be
   substituted)
½ cup granulated sugar
2 tablespoons arrowroot†
1 teaspoon lemon juice

STREUSEL TOPPING
¾ cup White Lily all-
   purpose flour
⅓ cup firmly packed
   brown sugar
Pinch of salt
6 tablespoons unsalted
   butter
¼ cup rolled oats

Tart Filling

Toss the blackberries in the granulated sugar, arrow-root, and lemon juice. Set aside.

Streusel Topping

Combine flour, brown sugar, salt, butter, and oat-meal in a food processor fitted with a metal blade. With pulsing switches, process mixture until the butter is the size of large peas. Set aside until ready to bake. Streusel can be made up to a week in advance if stored in the refrigerator.

Lightly flour rolling surface, the rolling pin, and the top of the Sweet Pastry Dough with all-purpose flour. Gently roll the dough ⅛-inch thick by rolling from the middle of the dough out. After each set of 2 rolls give the dough a quarter turn and re-flour surface area, dough, or rolling pin if needed. Once dough is completely rolled out, roll the dough back onto the rolling pin and slide the one, 9-inch fluted tart pan (with removable bottom) on to the middle of your work surface. Gently roll out the dough over the tart pan and then press the dough gently against the pan, evenly from the middle of the pan up to the sides of the pan. Roll the rolling pin over the top of the dough to break off any extra dough. Prick holes in the bottom of the dough with a fork and place in freezer for 5 minutes. Take out dough and place aluminum foil over it filled with pie weights or beans. Place in oven to "blind bake‡" for 15 minutes. When dough is finished "blind baking" the dough should be set and a light golden brown in color. Take out dough, remove aluminum foil and pie weights, and put back into the freezer for another 5 minutes.

Take out of the freezer and spread with the mas-carpone cheese mixture. Bake for 5 minutes or until set. Place back into the freezer to cool and to allow the mascarpone cheese mixture to form a seal between the crust and the berry mixture.

Take out the crust from the freezer and pour in the blackberry mixture. Top with the streusel topping. Bake 30 minutes or until bubbly. Cool. Serve warm. The Blackberry Streusel Tart will keep in the refrigerator for 2 days, but is best served warm from the oven.

*Chef's Note: Cornstarch can be substituted for arrowroot. In the tart filling section mix the cornstarch with the sugar before adding the lemon juice and blackberries.

**Blind baking is a term for baking the piecrust before it is filled. The process involves pricking the dough, covering the pie dough with parchment paper or foil, placing pie weights or beans on top, and then baking for 30 minutes or until the dough is cooked through. The foil should be removed in the last few minutes of baking to allow the crust to brown.

Blackberry Cornmeal Cobbler

This dish is our nod to the classic blackberry dessert. Summer just wouldn't be the same without a great cobbler. The best presentation of this dessert is in an impressive earthenware dish delivered bubbling to the table where everyone can dish out their own appropriately oversized portion. However, this recipe is easily produced as several individual portions. Whatever you do, don't forget the obligatory ice cream. I suggest our Bourbon White Chocolate Ice Cream, but no one will complain if you simply serve vanilla. *1 cobbler*

Preheat oven to 375° F.

Blackberry Filling

Toss the blackberries in granulated sugar, brown sugar, lemon zest, cinnamon, nutmeg, cornstarch, and dark rum. Place in a lightly greased 13×9×2-inch (3-quart) pan.

Topping

Cream butter and confectioner's sugar on low, to first incorporate the sugar into the butter and then on high, scraping often the sides of the bowl.

Add the eggs individually until well incorporated and cream until fluffy and a light yellow in color. Continue to scrape down the sides of the bowl, so that every ingredient is evenly mixed and properly aerated.

Combine flour, masa harina, cornmeal, baking powder, baking soda, and cloves. Add the dry ingredients into the butter and egg mixture, alternating with the buttermilk. Mixture should be thick, so that it can be piped.

Using a piping bag, pipe the batter onto black-

BLACKBERRY FILLING
- 6 cups blackberries
- 1 cup granulated sugar
- ½ cup packed brown sugar
- 2 each lemons, zested and minced or grated
- 1 teaspoon ground cinnamon
- 1 teaspoon ground nutmeg
- 1½ tablespoons cornstarch
- 1 tablespoon dark rum

6 tablespoons
   (or ¾ stick) butter
¾ cup confectioner's
   sugar
1 egg, room temperature
¾ cup all purpose flour
¾ cup masa harina
½ cup cornmeal
1½ teaspoons baking
   powder
½ teaspoon baking soda
¼ teaspoon ground
   cloves
Pinch of kosher salt
½ cup buttermilk

berries in a trellis pattern using a pastry bag with a tip. Bake until crust is browned and fruit is bubbling, about 30 to 35 minutes. Cool slightly before serving. This cobbler is best eaten the day it is made, just minutes from the oven.

Chef's Note: We use masa harina in several of our baking recipes that are oriented to the flavors of corn. Masa harina is the corn flour used in making tortillas and you will most often find it in the Mexican food section of your grocery store. I prefer it for many applications because of its fine texture compared to our stone ground cornmeal. If you cannot find it, you may substitute a ratio of 2 parts flour and 1 part cornmeal.

In addition, cloth and plastic piping bags are available at your local kitchen supply store. Refer to pages 47–48 for additional piping tips.

Blackberry Croissant Bread Pudding

As you might imagine, buttery croissants make a great base for
bread pudding. Again the bright flavors of blackberry are paired with rich
vanilla mascarpone. This is a great dessert to make a day before entertaining.
Just warm it before serving and serve with ice cream or simply whipped cream.
The Blueberry Lime Sauce we serve it with is a bright contrast to
this rich dessert. *Serves 6 to 8.*

Blackberry Croissant Bread Pudding
Preheat oven to 375° F.
Butter a standard 9x5x3-inch loaf pan.

Custard
Bring milk and sugar to a boil. Crack eggs into a
medium mixing bowl and slightly whip. Slowly
whisk hot milk and sugar mixture into eggs, being
careful not to curdle the eggs, and strain through a
fine-meshed strainer.

Blackberries
Combine berries, sugar and wine in a small
saucepan. Bring to a boil and remove from heat.
Let stand to cool.

Vanilla Mascarpone
Combine mascarpone, sugar, vanilla bean scrapings,
vanilla, and salt in a small bowl and whisk until
smooth in consistency.

CUSTARD
2¼ cups milk
½ cup sugar
4 large eggs

BLACKBERRIES
1½ cups blackberries
⅓ cup plus 1 tablespoon
  sugar
½ cup blackberry wine
  or ⅛ cup blackberry
  brandy

VANILLA MASCARPONE
8 ounces mascarpone
  cheese
1½ teaspoons sugar
½ vanilla bean, *scraped*
1½ teaspoon vanilla
  extract
Pinch of salt
6 baked day-old* large
  croissants

Makes 1 cup
2 cups blueberries
½ cup sugar
1 cup water
2 limes, zested,
1 lime, juiced

BUTTERMILK ICE CREAM
Makes 2 quarts
1 quart half and half
  cream
2 vanilla beans, split
1 tablespoon vanilla ex-
  tract
1 cup light corn syrup
12 egg yolks
10 ounces sugar
2 cups buttermilk

Blueberry Lime Sauce

Combine blueberries, sugar, water, lime zest, and juice in small saucepan. Bring this mixture to a boil, then reduce the heat to a slow simmer. Let this reduce until it coats the back of your spoon. Cool and serve at room temperature. This sauce, when poured, should not run, but hold its place on the plate.

Buttermilk Ice Cream

Combine half and half, vanilla beans, extract, and corn syrup and bring it to a boil in a medium saucepot. (Watch this carefully when it is close to boiling. It will easily boil over.) Remove from the heat and set aside.

Whisk together sugar and egg yolks in a large mixing bowl. **Temper in hot half and half mixture into the egg and sugar mixture. Return the mixture to the saucepot and put on medium heat, stirring constantly. Stir until the mixture begins to get thick and willl coat the back of a spoon. Remove from the heat and strain through a fine-meshed strainer into a stainless-steel vessel sitting in an ice bath. Stir in buttermilk. Allow ice cream base to cool completely. Spin ice cream according to the manufacturer's instructions of your ice cream machine.

To Assemble

Split croissants, soak in custard for 5 to 10 minutes.

Line the buttered loaf pan with croissant halves, inside facing out on top and bottom and all sides. Line the bottom with half of the berries. Pipe half of the mascarpone on top of the berries. Top mascarpone with soaked halves of croissants and repeat for one more layer. Sprinkle the top with sugar.

Bake at 375°F, for 30 minutes, or until blackberries are bubbling and the top is golden brown. Let stand for 30 minutes, then unmold by carefully running a knife along the sides and flipping it over onto a cutting board.

Serve slightly warm with Blueberry Lime Sauce and Buttermilk Ice Cream.

The Blackberry Croissant Bread Pudding will keep for 2 or 3 days in the refrigerator.

Chef's Note: Make sure your croissants have the chance to dry out for a day. If they don't, they will be too tender, and disintegrate when soaking in the custard.

**Culinary Tip: Tempering in this recipe is the process of carefully incorporating a hot liquid into uncooked eggs, allowing the eggs to incorporate without scrambling.*

The easiest way to accomplish this is to have someone whisk the eggs while you slowly pour in a stream of some of the hot liquid. Once the eggs have adjusted to the hot temperature of the liquid you can begin to pour in your liquid at a faster rate, while still whisking. Continue to whisk until all the hot liquid is incorporated into the eggs.

Bourbon White Chocolate Ice Cream

The combination of créme anglaise custard and sabayon custard make this a double-rich ice cream. The extraordinary richness is a perfect balance to your favorite bourbon in the ice cream. Don't use something you wouldn't drink! *Makes 1 Quart*

Bourbon Sabayon

Whisk yolks and sugar until well blended. Stir in bourbon. Whisk vigorously over a simmering water bath, until thick and pale yellow. Remove from heat and chill completely.

White Chocolate Ice Cream

Put the white chocolate in a medium bowl. Bring the heavy cream to a simmer and pour over finely chopped white chocolate.

Bring milk to a simmer. Combine egg yolks and sugar. Temper milk into egg and sugar mixture. Pour mixture into a saucepot and cook over medium heat, stirring constantly, until the mixture thickens and coats the backside of a spoon (if you have a kitchen thermometer this will be at about 180°F). Immediately remove the custard from the heat and strain, using a fine-mesh strainer, into a stainless-steel container that is sitting in an ice bath. Stir to cool custard.

Stir corn syrup and crème de cacao into the strained custard. Fold in the melted white chocolate and cream.

Fold the Bourbon Sabayon into the White Chocolate Ice Cream. Freeze according to the manufacturer's instructions of your ice cream machine.

BOURBON SABAYON
2 egg yolks
¼ cup granulated white sugar
2½ tablespoons bourbon

WHITE CHOCOLATE ICE CREAM
6 ounces white chocolate, finely chopped
1½ cups heavy cream
1 pint whole milk
⅓ cup plus 2 tablespoons (3 ounces) granulated white sugar
5 egg yolks
¼ cup corn syrup
2 tablespoons crème de cacao

Chef's Note: Another note on ice cream- I would refer to this preparation of ice cream as double rich. This method of enriching a traditional ice cream base, otherwise known as crème anglaise, with a flavored sabayon is a method that works very well for many types of ice creams. The sabayon is not only a way to incorporate a flavor, like bourbon, but it also contributes a sinful combination of whipped air and the richness of the egg yolks.

Blackberry Beverages

Blackberry Iced Tea

This is a refreshing version of the wine of the south, sweet tea.
This is definitely something for sipping by the pool or on the back porch
on a hot August night. *Makes 2 quarts.*

Place large tea bags, mint sprig, blackberries, sugar, and baking soda in a sturdy 2-quart glass pitcher. Pour the boiling water over all ingredients. Remove tea bags after 3 minutes.

Let sit at room temperature for 1 hour, and then strain. Stir to make sure all the sugar has dissolved. Add cold water to fill the pitcher. Allow the tea to come to room temperature before serving. Otherwise your tea will melt your ice cubes.

Add desired amount of ice and a wedge of lemon or lime.

Chef's Note: One of the first people I ever met at Blackberry Farm, Missy Whitehead, is an expert sweet tea brewer. She shared her grandmother's trick of adding a pinch of baking soda to tea to take away the bitterness.

2 large, family-sized tea bags
1 sprig large fresh mint
3 cups fresh or frozen, thawed blackberries crushed
2 cups granulated sugar
1 pinch baking soda
1 quart boiling water
1 cup cold water

Blackberry Vodka

This technique is an excellent way to capture the essence of blackberries at their peak. Use this as a base for some of the following cocktails—or let your imagination run with your own creations. *Makes 1 Fifth*

Place blackberries in a 2-quart jar. Pour vodka over blackberries. Cover tightly and keep at room temperature for 4 days. Turn the jar over every day. Transfer jar to the freezer and allow vodka to sit for at least one week. In the freezer it will last up to one year. Strain. You may use Blackberry Vodka in a variety of drinks.

Blackberry Cosmopolitan (Makes 1 drink)

Shake Blackberry Vodka, Cointreau or Triple Sec, lime juice, and cranberry juice with ice. Serve up in a chilled cocktail glass. Garnish with a large, fresh blackberry and a lime wedge or a twist of lemon.

Blackberry Martini (Makes 1 drink)

In a shaker filled with ice, add 2½ ounces Blackberry Vodka and ½ ounce Stoli Vanilla Vodka. Shake and pour into a chilled martini glass. Garnish with frozen blackberries.

Chocolate Blackberry Martini (Makes 1 drink)

In a shaker filled with ice, add 2 ounces of Blackberry Vodka and 1 ounce of Godiva Dark Chocolate Liqueur. Shake and pour into a chocolate-dipped martini glass (dip martini glass in melted chocolate, place glass in freeezer upside down on parchment paper for 10 minutes). Garnish with frozen blackberries.

BLACKBERRY VODKA
1 fifth vodka
1 pint fresh or frozen, thawed blackberries

BLACKBERRY COSMOPOLITAN
2 ounces Blackberry Vodka
1 ounce Cointreau or Triple Sec
½ ounce lime juice
1 ounce cranberry juice cocktail
Garnish: Fresh blackberries, lime or lemon wedges

BLACKBERRY MARTINI
2½ ounces Blackberry Vodka
½ ounce Stoli Vanilla Vodka
Garnish: two frozen blackberries

CHOCOLATE BLACKBERRY MARTINI
2 ounces Blackberry Vodka
1 ounce Godiva Dark Chocolate Liqueur.
Garnish: chocolate-rimmed glass, two frozen blackberries

Blackberry Kir Royale

The kir is king of Champagne-based apertifs. This is our own blackberry twist. Passing a tray of these beautiful deep rose-colored flutes is a great way to start a dinner party. *Makes 8 drinks*

Pour the Champagne into 8 flutes. Add a dash or two of blackberry brandy to each glass and garnish with a blackberry.

KIR ROYALE
1 bottle dry champagne (or sparkling wine)
¼ cup blackberry brandy
8 fresh blackberries

Blackberry Mint Julep

I am not typically a fan of the combination of blackberries and mint. But there is something about bourbon that brings them together magically. Try this next Derby Day or any hot summer day. *Makes 6 drinks*

Preheat oven to 200°F.

Line a baking sheet with parchment paper and arrange 1 cup of blackberries in a single layer.

Bake until the berries are dry and brittle. Cool, and then grind in a spice grinder.

Add sugar to taste, about 3 parts sugar to 1 part blackberry powder.

In a food processor, puree the remaining blackberries. Transfer to a bowl and set aside.

In a small saucepan, combine ½ cup sugar with water. Place over medium-high heat until the sugar is dissolved. Remove simple syrup from the heat and cool.

For each drink, dip the rim of a tall, chilled glass in blackberry powder. Using the back of a spoon, mash 3 mint leaves with 1 tablespoon simple syrup in each glass. Fill the glasses with ice, and add 2 ounces bourbon and 1 tablespoon blackberry puree to each glass. Stir. Garnish with a mint sprig and serve.

MINT JULEP
1 pint fresh blackberries
24 fresh mint leaves
12 ounces bourbon
1¼ cup sugar
½ cup water

Sources

Benton's Smoky Mountain
Country Hams
Country ham, bacon, sausage
   2603 Highway 411 North
   Madisonville, TN 37354
   (423)442-5003

Bridge Kitchenware Corp.
Kitchen equipment
   www.bridgekitchenware.com
   214 East 52nd Street New York, New
   York 10022
   (212) 688-4220
   Fax (212) 758-5387

Chef Revival USA, Inc.
Chef uniforms, equipment
   www.chefrevival.com
   22 Industrial Road
   Lodi, NJ 07644
   (973) 916-2060
   Fax (973) 916-6680

Chefwear
Chef uniforms
   www.chefwearusa.com
   311 North Knox
   Chicago, IL 60641-5200
   (800) 568-2433
   Fax (773) 427-8665

Cooks Illustrated Magazine
Expert advice on cooking, techniques, products
   www.cooksillustrated.com
   P.O. Box 7446
   Red Oak, IA 51591-0446
   (800) 526-8442

Falls Mill
Stoneground cornmeal, grits, flours
www.fallsmill.com
   134 Falls Mill Road
   Belvedere, TN 37306
   (931) 469-7161

The Great Smoky Mountain Roasting
Company
Specialty coffee
   Neil J. Crateau
   email: tncoffee@bellsouth.net
   9411 Northshore Drive
   Knoxville, TN 37922
   (865) 692-8717
   Fax (865) 692 8718

New York Cake and Baking Distribution
Pastry and baking equipment
   56 West 22 Street
   New York, NY
   (212) 675-CAKE
   Fax (212)675-7099

Pastry Arts and Design Magazine
The latest news in the world of pastry
> www.pastryartanddesign.com
> P.O. Box 333
> Mt. Morris, IL 61054
> (815) 734-1109

The Royal China and Porcelain
Companies, Inc.
For Lavinia and Evesham China
> WWW.ROYALCHINA.COM
> 1235 Glen Avenue
> PO Box 1012
> Moorestown, NJ 08057-0912
> (800) 631-7120
> Fax: (856) 866-2499

Muddy Pond Sorghum Mill
Sorghum
> 4363 Muddy Pond Road
> Monterey, TN 38574
> (931) 445-3589
> Fax: (931) 445-3589

Summerfield Farm
Free-range veal, lamb
> www.summerfieldfarm.com
> 10044 James Monroe Highway
> Culpeper, VA 22701
> (540) 547 9600
> Fax: (540) 547-9628

Sweetwater Valley Farm
Tennessee cheeses
> www.sweetwatervalley.com
> 17988 West Lee Highway
> Philadelphia, TN 37846
> (877) 862-4332
> (877) 862-4333 fax (865) 458-9221

Tennessee Valley Wine
Blackberry wine, Muscadine wine
> www.tennesseewines.com
> 15606 Hotchkiss Valley Road.
> East Loudon, TN 37774
> (423) 986-5147
> 888-TVW-WINE

White Lily Flour
Soft winter wheat, biscuit flour, plain and self-rising
> www.whitelily.com
> 218 East Depot Street.
> Knoxville, TN 37917
> (423) 546-5511

Acknowledgments

It is the team at Blackberry Farm that make my work such a delight everyday. Without them the enterprise would be just another hotel rather than the best place to work and to visit.

One of those people in particular deserves my deepest appreciation and gratitude for making this project a reality. Jenny Shepherd contributed countless hours and great patience, writing and testing recipes, editing and providing creative energy to this project. Jenny, it is people like you that make Blackberry Farm the most wonderful little hotel in the world.

JF

Also from Blackberry Farm Press

Teensy at Blackberry Farm